SHORT VISIT, LONG STAY

Brian Moses lives in Sussex with his wife and has two daughters. As a former teacher he has led many school trips and at the end of each one, vowed he'd never do another (but always did!).

Lucy Maddison lives in Streatham, London, with her partner Brian, daughters Sami and Katrina and an excitable hamster called Patch. She has very fond memories of school trips. Then again, never trust anyone over twelve!

SHORT VISIT, LONG STAY

School-trip Poems chosen by

BRIAN MOSES

Illustrated by Lucy Maddison

MACMILLAN CHILDREN'S BOOKS

For Liz, Tim, Philippa and Luke

First published 1998 as *School Trips* by Macmillan Children's Books

This edition published 2011 by Macmillan Children's Books
a division of Macmillan Publishers Limited
20 New Wharf Road, London N1 9RR
Basingstoke and Oxford
Associated companies throughout the world
www.panmacmillan.com

ISBN 978-1-4472-0020-8

3 5 7 9 8 6 4 2

A CIP catalogue record for this book is available from the British Library.

Printed and bound by CPI Group (UK) Ltd, Croydon, CR0 4YY

'Beware!' by June Crebbin first published in *The Jungle Sale* by Puffin Books.
'School Outing' by Gareth Owen first published in *My Granny is a Sumo Wrestler*
by Collins Children's Books.

CONTENTS

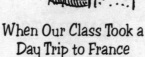

The Museum Trip

'Here we are, children.
The Museum!'
(Miss Protheroe, teacher, rubs her hands together in glee.)
'In we go.
This way, everybody.
Shshshsh!
Quiet!
Just look at that carving.
A lost art.
Observe those statues.
The craftsmanship!
Oh! Look! Hieroglyphics.
Study them, children.
Study them.
Children???'
The children have gone!
Miss Protheroe rushes here and there in a panic.
She can see it all in the papers the next day.
The headlines.
'WHOLE CLASS VANISHES. TEACHER BLAMED.'
Miss Protheroe goes hot all over.
Where are the children?
They are with the mummies.
No. Not their mummies.
The mummies.
They are gathered round a glass case gloating ghoulishly.
Oh, those musty wrappings.
That black, shrivelled arm.
They are faint with delight.
This is what *they* have come to see.

Marian Swinger

Amazing

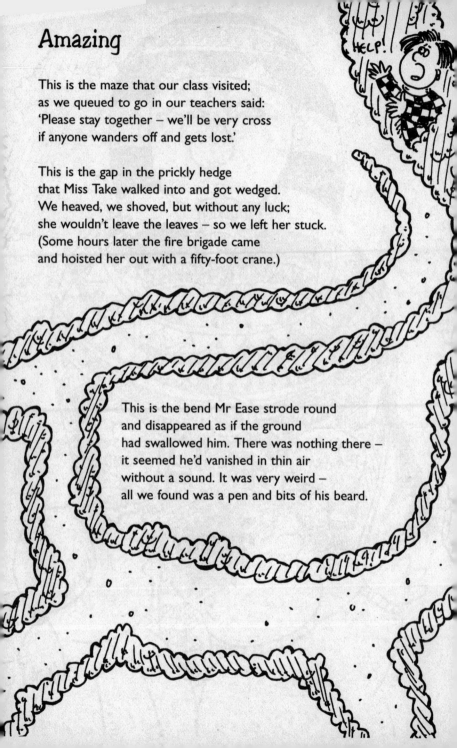

This is the maze that our class visited;
as we queued to go in our teachers said:
'Please stay together — we'll be very cross
if anyone wanders off and gets lost.'

This is the gap in the prickly hedge
that Miss Take walked into and got wedged.
We heaved, we shoved, but without any luck;
she wouldn't leave the leaves — so we left her stuck.
(Some hours later the fire brigade came
and hoisted her out with a fifty-foot crane.)

This is the bend Mr Ease strode round
and disappeared as if the ground
had swallowed him. There was nothing there —
it seemed he'd vanished in thin air
without a sound. It was very weird —
all we found was a pen and bits of his beard.

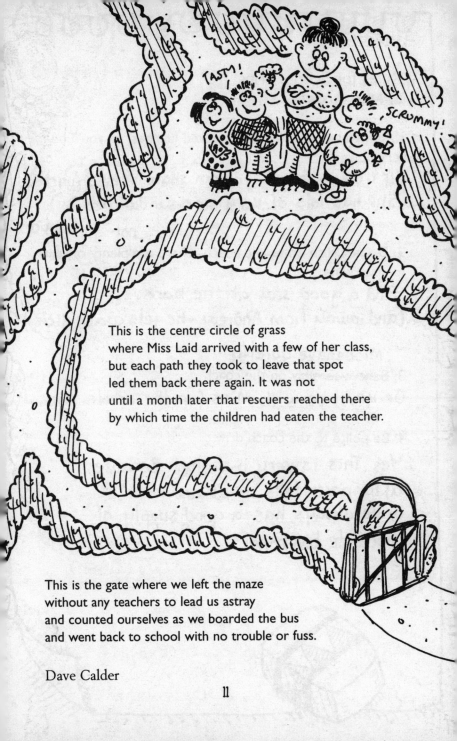

This is the centre circle of grass
where Miss Laid arrived with a few of her class,
but each path they took to leave that spot
led them back there again. It was not
until a month later that rescuers reached there
by which time the children had eaten the teacher.

This is the gate where we left the maze
without any teachers to lead us astray
and counted ourselves as we boarded the bus
and went back to school with no trouble or fuss.

Dave Calder

Rules for School Trips
by ~~Miss~~ Angela

1. Remember to bring your packed lunches, or you'll be very hungry.

(If you do forget, you can share Miss's lunch. She has lots of very nice sandwiches.)

2. Do ~~not~~ rush on to the coach. There are 'not' plenty of 'good' seats for everyone.

Find a good seat at the back,
(and away from Andrew – he gets coach sick.)

3. ~~Behave sensibly~~ , Misbehave quietly on the coach.
Or you'll be with Miss for the whole trip.

4. Be polite to the coach driver.

Yes. This is very important. Because:
a) He never tells on us and
b) He always has a good supply of chocolate bon bons.

12

5. Keep your rubbish in your lunch box or put it in a bin.

(Any unwanted food will be swapped or eaten by Clare)

Fairly

6. Always act in a sensible manner.

(when an adult is looking.)

your own   a friend

7. Never rush off on ~~the trip~~ – stay with ~~your group at all times.~~ It's more fun.

difficult

8. Always ask ~~interesting~~ questions.

Try one of these :

a) But why? (and keep asking 'But why?')

b) Are you really sure about that?

c) Is that a fact?

Forget

9. ~~Remember~~ – you are representing your school. ~~We have to create~~ a good ~~image.~~ time!!!!

James Carter

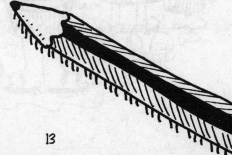

Same Again

School trip, school trip,
We're by the sea again,
And, just the same as last year,
It's pouring down with rain!

John Kitching

Diary of a School Trip

Day one
We arrive, it's pouring.

Day two
I'm still alive this morning.

Day three
Got sopping wet canoeing.

Day four
I'm now ashoo-ing.

Day five
Stuck sniffling in the dorm.

Day six
I wanna go back home!

Day seven
Wobbly like a welly
with my socks all wet and smelly
I'm heading back
along the track
to Home and What's On Telly.

Matt Simpson

A Teacher's Prayer

(On the night before a school trip)

Please deliver us from children
who can never sit still,
and spare us from small boys
who wander at will.

Please make sure our driver
might know the right way,
and could Bruiser our bully
be absent all day?

Please save us from swearing
and journeys too long,
please silence all first years
if they should burst into song.

Please watch over worksheets
so they stay by my side.
Please help me to cope.
Please be my guide.

And finally, one last thing,
before I fall into bed,
couldn't another teacher
please go instead?

Andrew Collett

Poor, Old Driver

Poor, old driver,
Front of the bus,
Can't stand the noise,
Hates all the fuss.

Icy road,
Fearing skids,
Only one thing worse –
Screaming kids!

John Kitching

Short Visit, Long Stay

The school trip was a special occasion
But we never reached our destination.
Instead of the Zoo
I was locked in the loo
On an M62 Service Station.

Paul Cookson

When Our Class Took a Day Trip to France

'More chic and less cheek!' our teacher declared.
'This class needs some culture, a taste of French flair.'
So it's Paris 'allo! London derrière!
On our very first day trip to France.

Harassed in Paris, our schedule was tight.
Sir worried and hurried us past famous sights,
Catching fragments of Follies and bistro sound bites,
To give us a flavour of France.

Sir was a blur on the banks of the Seine,
A wild running commentary scorching down lanes,
With him pointing out places and shouting their names.
As we galloped behind him through France.

24

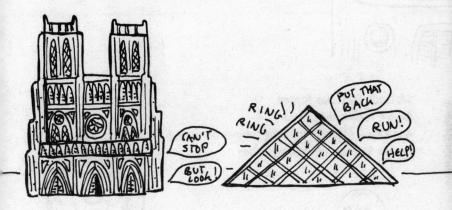

An eyeful of Eiffel was all that we got,
Then through Notre Dame we set off at a trot.
Did we see much of Paris? Well, no, not a lot.
We missed all the best bits of France.

Our Louvre manoeuvres set off the alarms.
We drew specs on Ms Lisa and ruined her charms.
We said it was Sir and they called the gendarmes.
(Do they still guillotine folk in France?)

Arm in arm with gendarmes, Sir stood on the quay.
We waved from the ferry as we put to sea.
Now he's in no hurry, Sir surely will see
A lot more than we did of France.

Maureen Haselhurst

School Outing

Class Four, isn't this wonderful?
Gaze from your windows, do.
Aren't those beauteous mountains heavenly?
Just drink in that gorgeous view.

Sir, Linda Frost has fainted
Aw Sir, I think she's dead
And Kenny Mound's throwing sandwiches round
I've got ketchup all over my head.

Oh, aren't these costumes just super?
Please notice the duchess's hat!
You can write up your notes for homework tonight,
I know you'll look forward to that.

Sir, Antoinette Toast says she's seen the ghost
Of that woman, Lady Jane Grey
And I don't know where Billy Beefcake is
But the armour is walking away.

So Sad

And here in this ghastly dungeon
The prisoners were left to die.
Oh, it's all just so terribly touching
I'm afraid I'm going to cry.

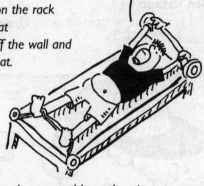

HELP!

Sir, Stanley Slack has put Fred on the rack
Sir, somebody's pinched your coat
Sir, Melanie Moreland's dived off the wall and
Is doing the crawl round the moat.

WONDERFUL DAY

Well, here we are, homeward bound again —
It's been a wonderful day.
I know when you meet your parents and friends
You'll have so many things to say.

Sir, what is that siren wailing for?
Sir, what's that road block ahead?
Sir, Tommy Treat is under the seat
Wearing a crown on his head.

Gareth Owen

Good Morning!

It's my first morning away from home
my first morning in this hotel
I slept really well, so did Teddy
once we had dropped off to sleep
around three in the morning
because Darren and Brett kept laughing
Ben was snoring
and James was whispering scary ghost stories
but now I'm awake

so I've put on my new jogging bottoms
my new T-shirt, my new jacket
my new gloves, my baseball hat
and my cagoule
I'm ready for anything, even though today
is the fourth of June
and the morning sun is shining over the sea
in flat golden patches
where the gulls bob and swoop
and cry like babies
and everywhere is still and calm and peaceful
mainly because
it's half past six in the morning
and breakfast isn't until eight o'clock
there's nothing to do
so I'll sing very loudly, wake everyone up
see if the teachers slept well like me.

David Harmer

CROC - O - DILES

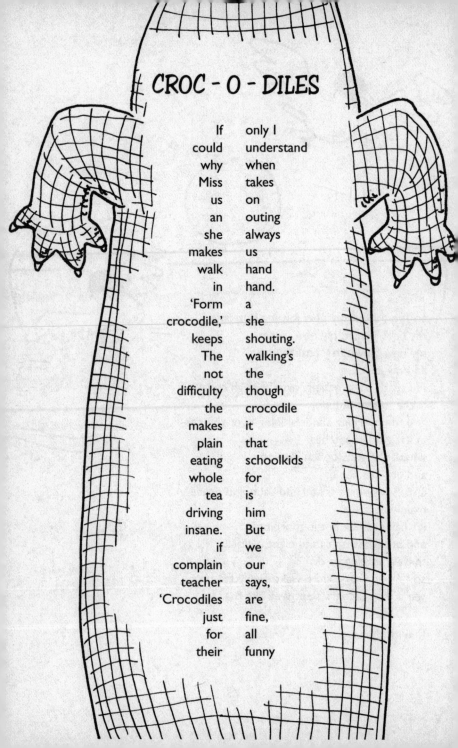

If only I
could understand
why when
Miss takes
us on
an outing
she always
makes us
walk hand
in hand.
'Form a
crocodile,' she
keeps shouting.
The walking's
not the
difficulty though
the crocodile
makes it
plain that
eating schoolkids
whole for
tea is
driving him
insane. But
if we
complain our
teacher says,
'Crocodiles are
just fine,
for all
their funny

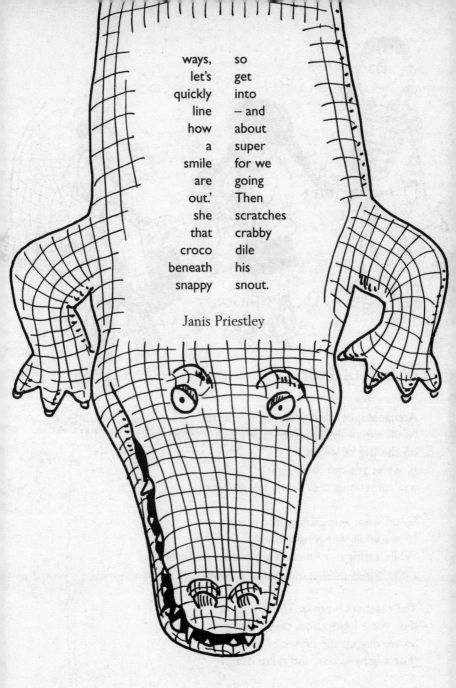

ways, so
let's get
quickly into
line – and
how about
a super
smile for we
are going
out.' Then
she scratches
that crabby
croco dile
beneath his
snappy snout.

Janis Priestley

Our Monster

Archaeologists find prehistoric animals
(well, bits of their skeletons at least)
on the Isle of Wight
(if we've got our facts right)
and sometimes they find a whole beast.

So off went our class to the island
to see what was lying around.
While eating our lunch in a meadow we noticed
some bones poking out of the ground.

The teachers were in The Red Lion.
(For voice lubrication, they'd said.)
So we dug up the bones of this monster.
(Just a baby it was, and quite dead.)

Tom shoved the four legs up his T-shirt,
and Emma hid teeth in her socks,
while Jan dumped the skull in her school-bag,
and the tail in her empty lunch-box.

Big Ali looked fat as a barrel
with the skeleton's ribs round his chest.
But weirdest was Elvis
who'd hidden the pelvis and vertebrae
under his vest.

In school, in the classroom next morning,
we piled all the bits in a heap.
But Sir said they weren't prehistoric.
Just the leftover bones of a sheep.

But we believe Sir is mistaken.
We think it's a SHEEPy-o-saurus.
Or a ptero-WOOLLY-dactyl or suchlike.
Or a much rarer RAM-ickytorus.
Or have we been hoaxed
by a prankster who got there beforus?

Barry Buckingham

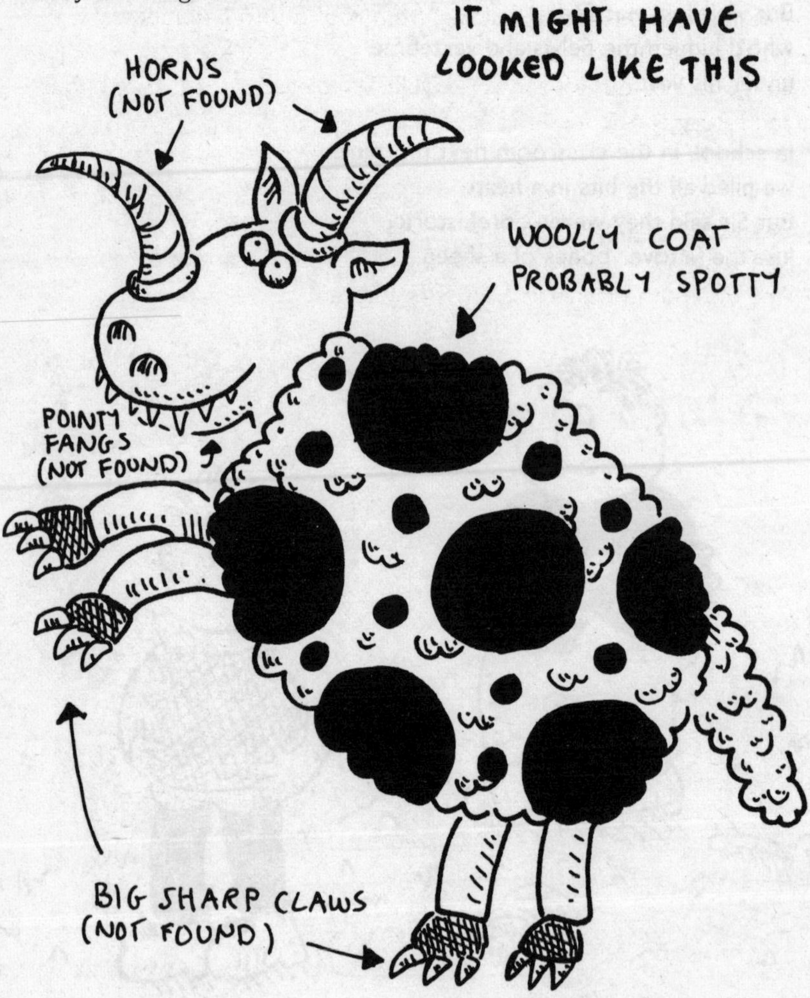

IT MIGHT HAVE LOOKED LIKE THIS

HORNS
(NOT FOUND)

WOOLLY COAT
PROBABLY SPOTTY

POINTY
FANGS
(NOT FOUND)

BIG SHARP CLAWS
(NOT FOUND)

Liam is Lost

'Form a straight line alongside the fossils;
I have an announcement to make.
We can't leave the museum until we find Liam,
However long it may take.

'We'll search the whole building, from roof top to basement,
Every department and floor.
So divide into threes, and walk QUIETLY please,
and return to the fossils at four.'

So ordered Miss Hurst before striding away
To the relics of Iron Age Man.
The other two teachers veered off to 'Stuffed Creatures',
And the mothers checked 'How Life Began'.

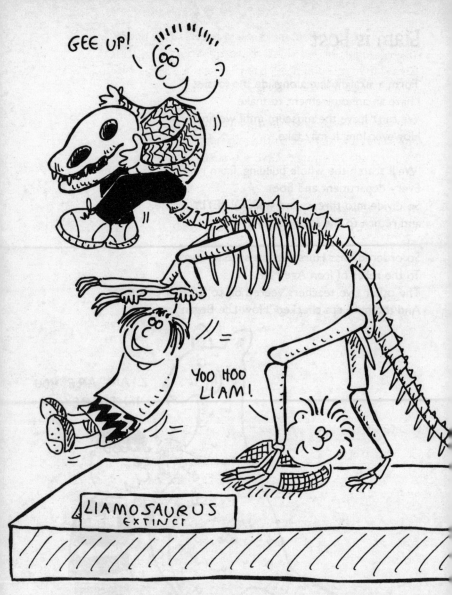

Then the kids all abandoned their worksheets and cheered.
At last they were free to explore!
They started to run and do cartwheels for fun,
And to gallop from floor to floor.

Class One played 'Peep-po' around huge marble pillars.
Class Two just played chase round the doors.
Class Three raced in pairs, using lift versus stairs,
While Class Four tried to climb dinosaurs.

The lost boy was called on the intercom.
His name rang all through the museum:
Round stuffed kangaroos, and the queues for the loos.
Yet the kids half forgot about Liam.

Then at four the school lined up to report.
One teacher had found a girl's shoe.
The mothers had Roy – alas, the wrong boy.
But Miss Hurst had discovered a clue:

A note in her handbag from Liam's own mum –
'My son has a cold and can't come.'

Kate Williams

Jason, who got his Head Stuck

Jason, who got his head stuck between railings,
in the Underground Works
on a trip to Dover Castle,
was merely demonstrating
how invaders could be repelled.
It was easy, he said,
all you had to do was slip between the bars.
But they must have been thinner
in days of old – trimmer of figure.
And although he was pushed and pulled and yanked,
Jason's head was firmly wedged.
'Step up on this ledge,' someone said.
'Let's lower the angle, dangle him down.
Perhaps we can tip him head over heels.'
But two loud squeals from Jason
proved we were wrong.
He was captured tight between two posts
and what hurt most wasn't physical pain,
it was everyone standing, jeering and laughing,
calling him daft to get himself trapped.
The safety officer wasn't happy,
he'd used up all of his patience today
on silly children who thought
they could play the invading army,
climbing the banks, barmy they were,
and now this. 'Stand aside, I'll fix it,'
he said, but nothing he could do
would budge Jason's head.
'Call the fire brigade,' someone said.

So two burly firemen levered apart
the railings where Jason had stuck.
'Next time,' his teacher said, as Jason
withdrew his head, 'next time,
we'll leave you there, like a criminal
in your pillory.' And Jason looked suitably
subdued till a TV crew popped up
from nowhere, to give him a moment
of glory, on the regional news that night.

Brian Moses

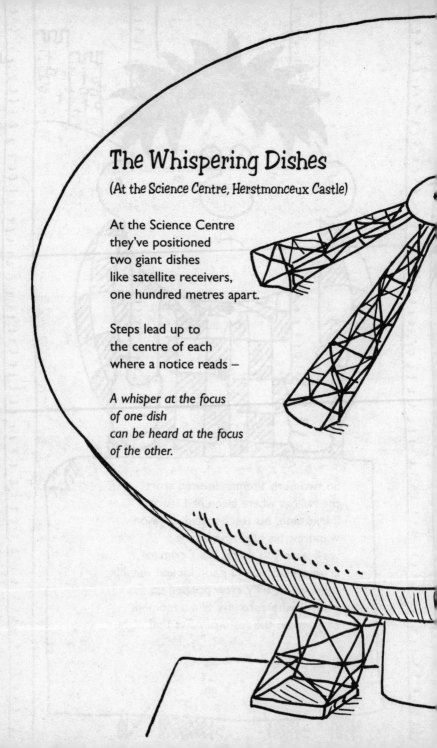

The Whispering Dishes

(At the Science Centre, Herstmonceux Castle)

At the Science Centre
they've positioned
two giant dishes
like satellite receivers,
one hundred metres apart.

Steps lead up to
the centre of each
where a notice reads –

*A whisper at the focus
of one dish
can be heard at the focus
of the other.*

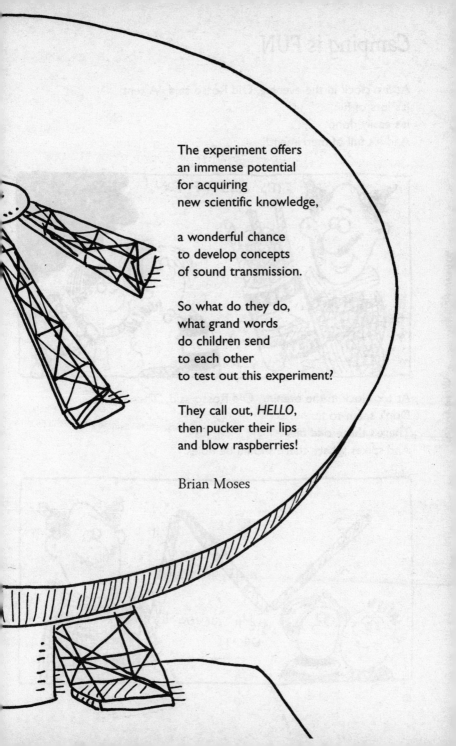

The experiment offers
an immense potential
for acquiring
new scientific knowledge,

a wonderful chance
to develop concepts
of sound transmission.

So what do they do,
what grand words
do children send
to each other
to test out this experiment?

They call out, *HELLO*,
then pucker their lips
and blow raspberries!

Brian Moses

Camping is FUN

At 5 o'clock in the evening, Old Rosso said, 'A tent!
It's lots of fun,
It's easily done
And it's full of merriment!'

At 6 o'clock in the evening, Old Rosso said, 'These poles
Don't seem to fit;
There's three odd bits
And spikes where there should be holes.'

At 7 o'clock in the evening, Old Rosso said, 'No pegs!
I'm really sure
I bought some more;
I think these pegs have legs!'

At 8 o'clock in the evening, Miss Johnson said, 'What's wrong?
It's getting late –
It's still not straight!
Are you sure it won't be long?'

At 9 o'clock in the evening, Old Rosso said, 'These ropes
Aren't long enough
And the ground's too tough:
That's why the whole thing slopes.'

At 10 o'clock in the evening, we settled down to sleep.
The ground was as hard
As the old school yard
When we started counting sheep.

At 11 o'clock in the evening, as the rain began to fall,
The wind found gaps,
There were flips and flaps
And it wasn't much fun at all.

Wheee! Creak! Wheee! Kerflumpp!

At 1 o'clock in the morning, we followed Mr Ross:
His merriment
Had all been spent
And we spent the night in the bus.

Trevor Millum

Five Things You Never Hear on a School Trip

I wish we were back in school doing sums.

It's a shame that there isn't enough room for *all* of the teachers to come with us.

FEELING GOOD!
LOOKING GOOD!

Don't teachers dress really well
when they're out on a school trip?

I can't wait until tomorrow!
That's when we'll spend all morning writing about our school trip!

MY SCHOOL TRIP
CHAPTER 5

I'm hungry. I wish I could sink my teeth into a scrumptious
school dinner.

Andrew Collett

YUM
YUM
SCHOOL
SLOP!

Mysteries of the Universe

We went by coach
to the planetarium
and saw the mysteries
of the Universe.

We saw the birth of stars,
black holes,
comets trailing cosmic dust,
and talked about
the existence of aliens.

But a greater mystery awaited us all.

When we left school
sixty-two of us boarded the coach.

When we arrived back at school
sixty-three of us got off.

Roger Stevens

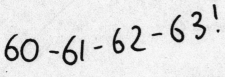

School Trip to Mars

As you know,
next month there is a school trip
to Mars.
We at Plumley Junior
are extremely proud
to be the first school in the world
to be chosen by NASA.
Unfortunately,
there are only two seats available.
We have put all the names in a hat.
The lucky children are
Brian Bully and Nancy Nuisance.
So, Brian and Nancy,
well done.
You will need your rough book
and colouring pencils –
and don't forget to take a packed lunch.
Everybody will be along
to send you off.
I expect there will be
a lot of emotion
from all your fellow pupils.
School just won't be the same
without you.
Oh yes,
please make sure
you take all your personal belongings home
before you go.

Charles Thomson

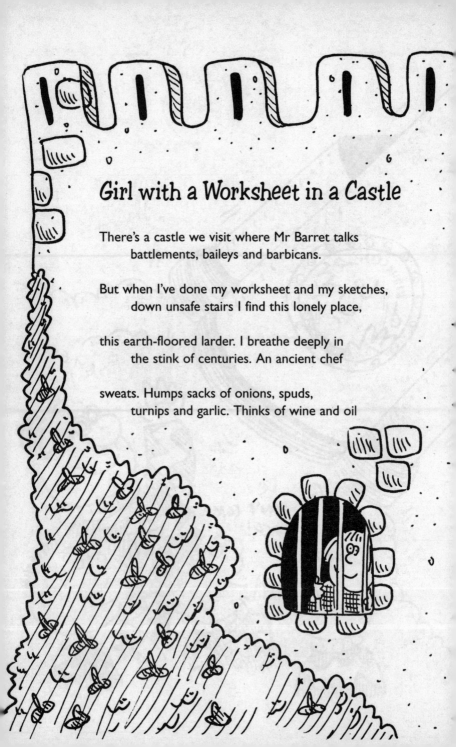

Girl with a Worksheet in a Castle

There's a castle we visit where Mr Barret talks
    battlements, baileys and barbicans.

But when I've done my worksheet and my sketches,
    down unsafe stairs I find this lonely place,

this earth-floored larder. I breathe deeply in
    the stink of centuries. An ancient chef

sweats. Humps sacks of onions, spuds,
    turnips and garlic. Thinks of wine and oil

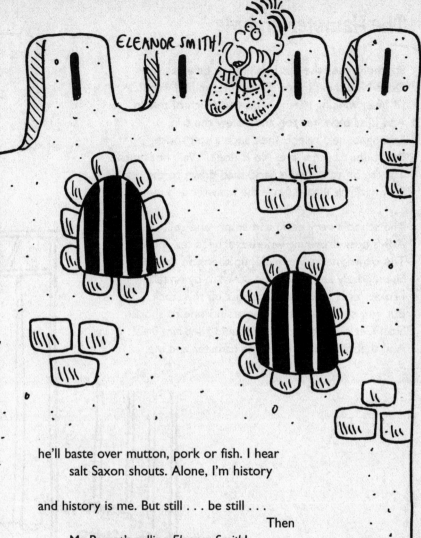

he'll baste over mutton, pork or fish. I hear
    salt Saxon shouts. Alone, I'm history

and history is me. But still . . . be still . . .
                                 Then
    Mr Barret's calling *Eleanor Smith*!

He asks me about battlements and baileys,
    and, not this lonely place, this worksheet.

Fred Sedgwick

The Hamster and Me

So, there goes the bus and I'm left behind.
Does Miss think I care? Does Miss think I mind?
I'd been winding her up – bit too much of the lip
And Miss blew her top and I blew the trip.
I thought she'd relent, she's such a soft touch,
But it don't bother me. No it don't. Well, not much.
They're off to a theme park, then down to the sea.
So what? We'll have fun – the hamster and me.

The school's very eerie and empty and still,
A fly's busy drowning where teacher's tea spilled.
The clown masks we made, up there on the shelf,
Seem grizzly and gruesome now I'm by myself.
I could mess up the sink, or mix up the stock,
But why should I bother, there's no one to shock?
Shall I let out the hamster? Should I set him free?
And then we'll have fun – the hamster and me.

He trundles his treadmill, it squeaks round and round
Like a tiny Big Wheel in the theme park fairground.
His claws skitter-scat as I open his door
And he hurries to hide in his stale yellow straw.
He's only pretending, he's trying to tease.
Come on out, hamster. Come on out, please.
Miss needn't feel guilty, she really should see
The fun that we're having – the hamster and me.

Maureen Haselhurst

Four School Trips

The most spectacular
was Mr Grindle our caretaker
catching his foot on the mop and bucket
left by Miranda, our school cleaner
who quickly came after
tangled up in the tubes of the hoover.

WHOA!

The most entertaining
was Mr Chigwell our headteacher
who stumbled over his feet as he carried
two big boxes of blue powder paint
three big boxes of red powder paint
four big boxes of white powder paint
a big tub of glue
and a bucket of water.

The most refreshing
was Mrs Grinch the chief dinner lady
stubbing her toe on a table leg
and tipping two large jugs of custard
over the head of my mate Martin
just as he stuck up his hand
for extra pudding.

The most embarrassing
was out on the playground
I was kicking a ball and lost my balance
fell into the arms of Kirsty and Kerry
who giggled and shrieked
at the top of their voices
I went red, everyone laughed
and called me Lover Boy all week.

David Harmer

Beware!

The crocodile is coming!
It's heading for the pool,
It's swaying down the road
From the local Primary School.
Better keep your distance,
Better close your doors –
Beware the fearful clamour
From its ever-open jaws!
Be careful not to stumble
As you hurry from the street:
Remember that the crocodile
Has sixty tramping feet!
Through the city jungle
The creature marches on.
Wisely, shoppers stand aside
And wait until he's gone.
It's going to cross the busy street –
It starts to leave the path –
Attacked by snarling traffic
It's completely cut in half –
The head continues on its way,
The tail, delayed, just laughs
And runs to catch it up
At the Municipal Baths.
The crocodile is swimming
In the Public Swimming Pool
But soon it will be heading
For the local Primary School.
So, better keep your distance,
Better if you try
To find a place to hide
While the crocodile goes by!

June Crebbin

School Trip of the Future

All right then kids, where shall we go?
Venus? Mercury? Mars?
Any one place in particular,
Or seventy different stars?

And once we're there just don't forget
What carelessness can cause –
You know what Kevin Thompson did
When he picked up all those spores,

Lodged in the heels of his trainers –
Killed half the population,
And then it cost a billion pounds
For World inoculation.

And don't bring any creatures back,
Like that Sharromog from Whatsit –
It ate New York and Tokyo
Before the army shot it!

And for heaven's sake don't miss the ship,
You know that it can't wait –
Simpson did on Planet Zob
And got back centuries late.

ARE YOU HIDING
SOMETHING, BEN?

And take your anti-ageing pills,
Not like Tony Black,
He lost his on that trip to Tard –
He was mummified when he got back.

61

And don't forget your suntan cream,
Stars are hot, you know.
Factor fifty thousand works –
It stops that burning glow.

And what about that gormless twit –
Alistair McCart –
He took his space-suit off last year
And blew himself apart.

MISS
I'M BORED

ONLY 1000
YEARS TO GO

And we don't want any fisticuffs
Like we've sometimes had before –
When some soft berk has been the cause
Of interstellar war.

And one last thing, if the fuel runs out,
Make sure you've brought plenty to do.
Bring a few books, a thousand or so –
We'll be up there a century or two . . .

Clive Webster